EVERYDAY SCIENCE

Fully Charged:
Electricity

Steve Parker

Heinemann
LIBRARY

Chicago, Illinois

For information, address the publisher:
Heinemann Library, 100 N. LaSalle, Suite 1200, Chicago, IL 60602
Customer Service: 888-363-4266
Visit our website at www.heinemannlibrary.com

Printed and bound in China by South China Printing Company.
08 07 06 05 04
10 9 8 7 6 5 4 3 2 1

Library of Congress Cataloging-in-Publication Data

Parker, Steve.
  Fully charged : electricity / Steve Parker.
     p. cm. -- (Everyday science)
Summary: Describes how electricity is generated, harnessed, and used,
and explains the difference between electricity, including static
electricity, and electronics.
  ISBN 1-4034-4813-2 (HC), 1-4034-6419-7 (PB)
  1. Electric engineering--Juvenile literature. 2.
Electricity--Juvenile literature. [1. Electric engineering. 2.
Electricity.] I. Title. II. Everyday science (Heinemann Library (Firm))

  TK148.P33 2004
  621.3--dc22

                                    2003014779

Acknowledgments
The publishers would like to thank the following for permission to reproduce
photographs: Alamy/Charlotte Wood/Arcblue p.44; Bang and Olufsen p.49;
Corbis p.24; Directphoto.org/Tom Craig p.5; Findphoto p.29; Fraser Photos p.15;
Getty Images/ BrandXPictures p.31; Getty p.4; Harcourt Index pp.8, 32, 48; OSF/
Ehrenstrom p.9; RobertHarding p.35; SPL p.11, 37, SPL/De Schwanberg p.7,
SPL/Tek Image p.10, SPL/ Wallick p.17, SPL/Bond p.18, SPL/ Morgan p.19,
SPL/Maximillian Stock p.21, SPL/ Adam Hart-Davis p.27, SPL/Alfred Paskieka
p.47, SPL/Gusto p.50, SPL/Rosenfeld Images Ltd p.52; The Flight Collection p.13;
Topham/Dawes p.43; Trip/Rogers p.14.

Cover photograph of a band perfoming on stage reproduced by permission of
Redferns/ Jim Sharpe.

Artwork: Art Construction p.51, Ascenders p.22; Jeff Edwards p.27; Mark
Franklin pp.7, 30, 36, 38, 41, 43; Visual Image p.25.

The publishers would like to thank Robert Snedden for his assistance in the
preparation of this book.

Contents

Electricity Everywhere

Probably no area of science and technology affects our everyday lives as much as electricity. It is with us all the time. It powers our machines and gadgets and helps us see and cook and keep warm. It carries us from place to place and drives our tools and appliances. It allows us to exchange news and information by phone and computer and makes our lives more comfortable.

Sound power
Personal music relies on electricity through wires to the earphones. The electrical energy comes from storage units called batteries.

Convertible

Electricity is the most important form of energy in the modern world, for several reasons. One is that it is convertible. It can be changed easily into many other forms of energy, such as light in bulbs and TV screens, sound in radios and music systems, warmth in various types of heaters, and motion in the electric motors that drive machines.

The world's biggest blackout

On August 14, 2003, the world's biggest electricity failure affected northeastern North America. At about 4:10 p.m. local time, the power outage paralyzed large cities such as Detroit, Cleveland, New York City, Toronto, and Ottawa. More than 60 million people were affected. They were stuck in elevators and subways. Huge traffic jams choked roads, and air-conditioning failed. The inconvenience dragged on for hours, in some areas even days. It was a spectacular demonstration of how much our modern world depends on electricity.

Variable

Electricity comes in many forms and amounts. We can make and use huge amounts of it, or small amounts. Electricity can be powerful enough to drive huge machines. Or it can flow in tiny quantities billions of times smaller, in electronic devices such as computer chips. Special devices such as transformers change electricity from strong to weak. Also, different power sources, from huge power plants to batteries smaller than this letter o, produce varied amounts of electricity.

Transportable

Another reason why electricity is so important in our lives is that it is transportable. It can be sent thousands of miles or kilometers across continents or under oceans. Electricity travels along wires and cables, from the places where it is produced, right into our homes. Imagine if the same amounts of energy were moved from place to place, but in forms other than electricity, such as coal or gasoline. We would need many more trucks, tankers, train cars, ships, planes, and other cargo-carriers.

Convenient

In addition to all this, electricity is convenient. It can be turned on and off at the flick of a switch. This makes it easy to stop and start the flow of electricity into a device or appliance. In fact, electricity can be switched on and off millions of times every second. This feature allows electricity to carry data or information. This is usually done in the form of a code. In digital techniques, electricity flows in patterns of stop-go signals. In the analog system, it flows in patterns of varying strength. Computers and information technology are built around this data-carrying feature of electricity.

Electric travel
This tram, like many other public transportation systems, runs on electricity.

What Is Electricity?

Electricity is familiar and useful, but what exactly is it? We cannot see electricity. We view its effects when it drives a motor or makes a light bulb shine. But an ordinary wire looks exactly the same whether it is carrying electricity or not. Likewise, we cannot really hear electricity itself. But we can hear the sounds produced when it powers a loudspeaker, or the crackle of sparks as it jumps through the air. We cannot smell electricity either, although we may detect an odor of burning that could warn us that an electrical device is overheating. The body can feel electricity passing through it. But this is one of electricity's greatest dangers, since the strength of the electricity from a wall socket in the home is powerful enough to kill a person.

Why electricity?

Over 2,500 years ago, ancient Greeks carried out experiments by rubbing pieces of amber (hardened, fossilized tree sap). This made the amber attract objects such as feathers. We now know this effect is a result of static electricity. The ancient Greek word for amber was *elektron*. In about 1600, English scientist William Gilbert did similar experiments. He adapted the Greek word to come up with the term *electric*.

Electricity as energy

One way of describing electricity is as a form of energy. Light, heat, and motion are also forms of energy. All types of energy have the ability to cause change and make things happen. This is the reason why electricity is so useful. But where does electricity come from?

Electricity and atoms

All matter is made up of atoms. Electrical energy comes from inside atoms. Atoms are so tiny that they can be seen only with a very powerful microscope. The dot on this letter *i* contains many more atoms than there are people in the world. Yet atoms are not the smallest known objects. Each atom is made of even tinier parts, known as subatomic particles. There are three main kinds of subatomic particle—protons, neutrons, and electrons.

Inside atoms

Protons and neutrons are clumped in the center, or nucleus, of an atom. Protons are positive—that is, they have what is known as a positive electrical charge. Neutrons are neutral, with no charge. Electrons are much smaller and lighter. They can be imagined as moving around and around the nucleus. They have a negative electrical charge. Normally an atom has the same number of protons and electrons. For example, an atom of the metal copper has 29 protons and 29 electrons. The 29 positive protons balance, or cancel out, the 29 negative electrons. As a result, the atom has no electrical charge.

Bright spark
Electricity sometimes flows through air, making the light and heat of a spark.

Electrons on the move

Usually the electrons stay in their atoms. But if they are given a small push, then in substances such as copper, they can jump from one atom to the next. When trillions of electrons do this, all hopping in the same direction, we call it a flow, or current, of electricity.

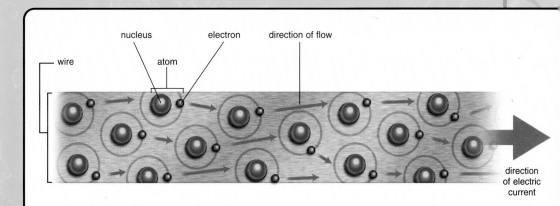

nucleus   electron   direction of flow

wire   atom

direction of electric current

Electric current
The arrows show the direction of flow of the stream of electrons that make up electric current as they jump from atom to atom.

Natural Electricity

If there were no people on Earth, there would still be electricity. It is a natural type of energy and exists in many places and forms. One of the most powerful forms is lightning. Lightning is a gigantic spark of electrical energy. It leaps through the sky, either between clouds, or from a cloud to the ground, and then perhaps back up again to the cloud (see page 13).

Nerves and electricity

Natural electricity is found inside the bodies of animals. It is produced and used in various ways. One use of electricity is as the tiny pulses we call nerve signals. All but the simplest animals have senses and a nervous system and brain. They use these systems to sense their surroundings and control their movements.

Making and sensing electricity

Electricity is also made in the muscles. As muscles work, they produce tiny surges of electricity. Electricity hardly passes through air at all, but it flows easily through water. In lakes, rivers, and seas, the invisible electrical ripples from an animal's working muscles pass out through the water, usually for a several feet. These weak, invisible ripples can be picked up by certain creatures, especially predators such as sharks and rays. A shark has tiny holes over much of its snout and head that can pick up electrical signals. The shark can sense nearby creatures by feeling the electricity they give off, even in total darkness or when the creature is buried in the mud.

Flying sparks
Lightning happens when a huge charge of electricity jumps from clouds to the ground and back.

Finding the way by electricity

Certain kinds of fish have much more complex and powerful electrical parts. Some of the muscles in the bodies of electric eels and rays act as "living batteries" that can produce electricity as well as movement. These fish constantly send out small electrical pulses, usually from the tail end. Sensors in the head pick up the pulses. An object nearby blocks them. These fish use their electrical sense to find their way in muddy water or at night. They also use it to detect prey—and perhaps kill it!

Guided by electricity

Scientists did an experiment to test how sharks use electricity to find food. At night, they lowered a short hollow rod into the water. The rod gave out a tiny electrical signal from one end, and the odor of meat from the other. The scent of the meat attracted many blue sharks from far away. But when the sharks approached the bait in the darkness, they made more than three-quarters of their strikes at the electrical end of the rod. This shows the importance of the shark's electrical sense, especially in darkness when they cannot use sight.

Electrical weapons

Electric eels and rays can use their electricity-making power as a deadly weapon. They can send out a pulse of electricity with a strength of 500 volts. This is several times more powerful than the electricity from the wall sockets in our homes. These fish use their electrical power to shock and stun prey or to defend themselves against enemies.

Danger fish
Electric rays and other fish that can produce surges of electricity are among the most dangerous underwater creatures.

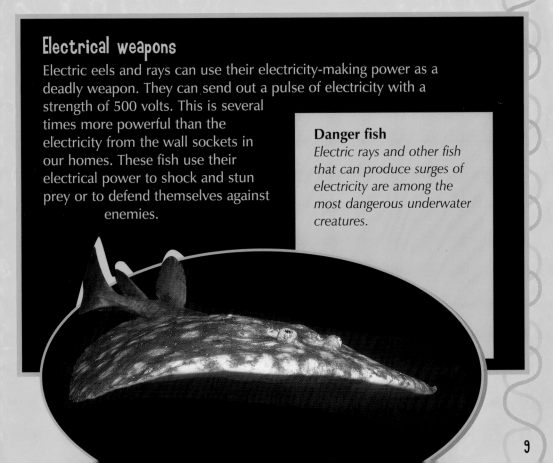

Human Electricity

The human body is full of electricity, but only in tiny amounts. This natural body electricity is made in two main ways. The first is as a by-product from the chemical processes that occur in working muscles.

The heart and ECG

A beating heart gives off very weak pulses of electricity. These pulses travel well through the whole body because most of the body is made of substances, such as water and dissolved chemicals, that conduct electricity easily. The heart's electrical pulses can be detected as they reach the skin by sensor pads stuck on various parts of the body. The pads feed the tiny waves of electricity along wires into a device called an electrocardiograph machine (ECG). The ECG displays them as a wavy line on a screen or strip of paper. The resulting ECG trace gives doctors valuable information about the health of the heart.

3 1833 04792 9952

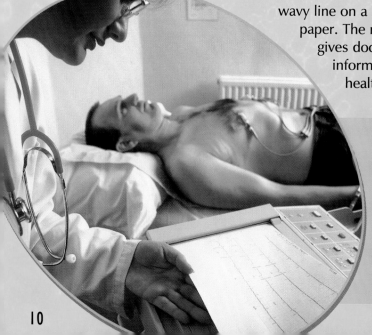

ECG testing
Doctors use ECG machines to check the condition of a patient's heart— the body's most important muscle.

The nervous system

Electricity also occurs in the body as nerve signals. A nerve signal is a tiny pulse of electricity. Its strength is less than one-tenth of a volt (15 times less than from a flashlight battery), and it lasts only one-thousandth of a second. Millions of these nerve signals flow along the body's nerves every second. The system carries information. It is the body's own "inner Internet." Nerve signals bring information from the eyes, ears, and other senses to the brain so we know what is happening around us. More nerve signals travel from the brain out to the muscles, to tell them when to work, so we can move around.

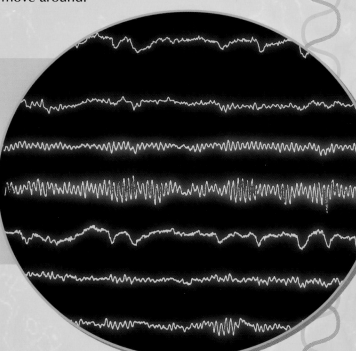

EEG display
Different patterns of electrical signals from the brain are picked up by sensor pads on different parts of the head. Taller waves closer together indicate greater brain activity.

The brain and EEG

The brain works using electricity. It receives and sends billions of nerve signals every second, to and from body parts. Our thoughts, ideas, and memories exist as nerve signals traveling along pathways around different parts of the brain. Even as we sleep, these electrical signals continue to flash back and forth through the brain and along nerves. They travel at speeds of more than 330 feet (100 m) per second. Like the electrical pulses from the heart, the brain's nerve signals can be detected using pads on the skin and displayed by a machine called an EEG, or electro-encephalograph. The spiky lines, or brain waves, provide doctors with information on how the brain is working and help to identify problems such as epilepsy, bleeding, or stroke.

Static Electricity

In daily life, we think of electricity as moving or flowing along a wire, in the same way that water flows along a pipe. This is only partly true. Many everyday gadgets use electricity that does not flow along smoothly. The electricity in them is stationary, or static. To understand how this can happen, it helps to look more closely at exactly what electricity is.

Collecting charge

In a Van de Graaff generator, static charge from the moving friction-belt is carried up to the dome. Then it leaps as a spark to the smaller sphere.

Charge!

As shown earlier, in an atom there are positive protons and negative electrons. Most atoms, most of the time, have the same number of electrons and protons. So the whole atom has no overall electrical charge. Various kinds of energy such as rubbing, magnetism, and heat can jolt an electron away from its nucleus. When this happens, the electron's negative charge is no longer balanced by the positive charge of a proton in the nucleus. The electron represents a unit of negative electrical charge, while the rest of the atom has a unit of positive electrical charge. This process is called separating charge. It is the basis of making electricity.

Rubbed-off charge

A common way of separating charge is by rubbing an object that does not carry flowing electricity well. Such substances include glass, rubber, and various types of plastic. The energy of the rubbing strips electrons from the atoms on the surface, creating positive and negative charges. Some substances lose electrons in this way and become negatively charged. Others gain electrons from the object they are rubbed against. These objects become positively charged. These charges stay still, or static, unless they have somewhere to flow. Common names for these charges include static electricity, static charge, and electrostatic charge.

Air to Earth

Before a plane is refueled, grounding straps (the green cables in the photo) are attached to it. They carry away the static electricity that the plane picks up in flight and direct it harmlessly into the ground. Then, as the fuel pipe connects, there is no danger of a spark leaping from the plane to it. This could otherwise cause the fuel to explode.

Discharge

If an object that carries electricity well comes near to or touches an object with static charge, the charge may suddenly move. It leaps to the other object, so the positives and negatives spread out and become balanced again. This leaping, known as discharge, is sometimes visible as a tiny flash of light, like a mini lightning bolt. It can happen when we walk on a carpet and our shoes rub on it, or while traveling in a car. Charge builds up on our bodies. When we touch an object that carries electricity well, such as a door handle, we feel the static charge discharge into it as a small electric shock.

Flash, bang

Lightning is a giant spark, or electrical discharge. In a thundercloud, billions of tiny water droplets and other particles swirl around in the strong winds. As the droplets and particles rub against one another, electrons are separated from their atoms. The free electrons have electrical charge. They increase in number until they have enough energy to jump at incredible speed to a place where they can spread out—usually the ground. As they do so, they heat the air and give off light, which we see as lightning. The flash is so hot, up to 54,000°F (30,000 °C), that it heats the air around it almost instantly. This causes the air to move faster than the speed of sound. The process of heating the air continues, spreading away from the giant spark as a boom of thunder.

Static Electricity in Everyday Life

In daily life, static electricity (electrical charge) can be very useful. It can be stored in parts called capacitors (condensers), which are used in many kinds of electrical equipment. Capacitors are usually made of metal plates separated by a narrow gap or a layer of a substance that does not conduct electricity. The sheets are either flat or wound into a spiral, like a tiny roll of aluminum foil. The charge is fed to the plate along a wire. It builds up there until it is needed, when it is allowed to flow away in a rush along another wire. The amount of charge a capacitor can store is called capacitance. It is measured in units called farads. One farad is a very large amount of charge. The charge held by capacitors in everyday electrical equipment is usually measured in microfarads (millionths of a farad).

When charge can damage

A flash of lightning is a huge amount of electrical energy. This electrical energy can pass through an object. When this happens, the object can be badly damaged, set on fire or even exploded. Lightning tends to hit the nearest or highest object. So tall buildings have large metal rods, straps, or ribbons running from their tops down into the ground. These are called lightning rods. They may be on the outside of the building, or contained safely within its structure. They carry the electrical charge safely down into the ground.

Taking charge
People protect buildings from lightning bolts with lightning rods, like the one shown here, to direct charge down into the ground.

Flash picture

Electricity has been used for years to power photo flash attachments. These devices give enough light to take good pictures in low light.

Smile please

One use of capacitors is in electronic flash attachments for cameras. The flash spends time charging—that is, building up charge in its capacitors, from the electrical energy in its batteries. When you press the button to take a picture, a sudden burst, or discharge, of electrical energy passes through the unit to make the flash of bright light that lasts a fraction of a second.

Tuning in

In a gasoline engine, short but powerful pulses of electricity are fed to the spark plugs. The spark plugs create sparks that make the fuel explode, or combust. In a car, these bursts of electricity from the engine can interfere with the car radio and make a crackling sound. This is because sparks make their own tiny amounts of radio waves. Capacitors in the engine's electrical system help to smooth out the crackling effects so that the radio picks up stations clearly. Many radios use capacitors themselves, in their tuning systems. The tuning knob is a variable capacitor. As it turns, it allows different amounts of charge to pass through. This enables the tuning system to pick up different radio stations.

The biggest charges

The amounts of charge in everyday electrical devices are tiny compared to the gigantic amounts used in scientific research. The biggest machines in the world are particle-accelerators, or atom-smashers. Some have tubes many miles or kilometers long. They are designed to give particles such as electrons huge amounts of energy, which make them reach amazing speeds—almost the speed of light. Then the particles smash into a target and break it, or themselves, into pieces. These experiments allow scientists to study the inner structure of atoms. There are practical benefits, too. Through these experiments, scientists have gained knowledge that has enabled inventors to come up with many kinds of machines and gadgets, from televisions to medical scanners.

Attract and Repel

Electrostatic charge is useful partly because an object with one type of charge pulls or attracts a nearby object with the opposite charge. So, a negatively charged item attracts a positively charged one. Two objects with the same charge repel, or push each other apart. The rule is that like charges repel, unlike charges attract.

Electricity and magnetism

The attraction and pushing apart of electrical charges works the same way as in magnetism. In magnetism, a positive (north) magnetic force attracts a negative (south) one and repels another positive one. In fact, electricity and magnetism are two features of the same basic force. This is called the electromagnetic force and is one of the most basic forces in the universe, as we will see. An invisible magnetic field surrounds a magnet and exerts a force on any magnetic object within it. In the same way, an object with an electrical charge is surrounded by an invisible electric field that affects nearby electrically charged objects.

Why do TV screens get dusty?

The inside of a traditional TV or computer screen is the target for billions of electrons every second. Devices called electron guns in the television fire the electrons. The electrons carry negative charges that gradually build up on both the inside and outside of the screen. The charged screen then attracts tiny bits of dust and other floating particles, especially those that naturally have a slight amount of opposite charge.

Copying with charge

Photocopying machines use electrostatic charge. The charge is on a large drum coated with the metal selenium. Light is shined onto the drum, in the pattern of the image to be copied. For darker parts of the image, less light, and for brighter parts, more light reaches the drum. Where light hits the drum, the light energy causes the charge to spread out. So the parts of the drum matching the bright areas of the image have less charge. Then a powder, called toner, with the opposite charge is added. The toner is attracted to the parts of the drum with most charge. Finally a sheet of paper rolls over the drum and picks up the toner.

Sprays and powders

Some kinds of sprays use static charge to give an even flow. As the particles of the spray leave the nozzle, they are all given the same charge. This means they repel each other, so they spread out evenly rather than clump together. Crop-sprayers and crop-dusters on tractors and planes work in this way. So do paint-sprayers used on cars and other large metal objects. The car is given an opposite charge so it attracts the paint droplets. As a result, less paint is wasted.

Fine spray
Static charge given to the millions of droplets from a crop-sprayer makes them spread out widely as a fine, even mist.

Cleaning the air

Other devices that rely on static charge are certain kinds of air filters. Dirty air, with bits of floating dust and other particles, passes through a mesh of wires charged with electricity. The wires give a charge to the passing particles. Then the air flows past another mesh with the opposite charge. The particles stick to this mesh, leaving the air cleaner. Air ionizers are designed to produce floating charged particles, called negative ions, in air. Some people think these ions have beneficial effects on the human body.

Flowing Electricity

Most of the electricity we use in our machines, gadgets, and appliances is moving electricity, called electric current or a flow of charge. It moves in a steady stream, just as water in a river flows as a steady current. The problem is, we can see and feel flowing water, but we cannot see electricity. It is more difficult to imagine its movement. However, comparing electricity to water helps to explain how we measure electricity. We use terms we often hear in connection with electrical machines and gadgets, such as volts and amps.

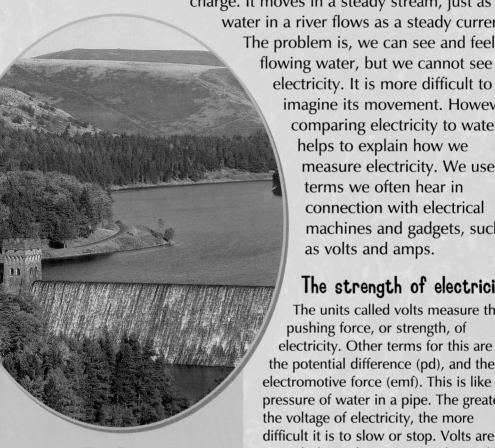

Controlling flow
Water and electricity have some similarities. This makes it easier to understand the features of electricity, since its flowing charge cannot be seen.

The strength of electricity

The units called volts measure the pushing force, or strength, of electricity. Other terms for this are the potential difference (pd), and the electromotive force (emf). This is like the pressure of water in a pipe. The greater the voltage of electricity, the more difficult it is to slow or stop. Volts are named after Italian scientist Alessandro Volta (1745–1827). He was one of the first people to make a source of steadily flowing electricity, in 1800. We would now call this a battery or electric cell. A typical flashlight battery has a low voltage, about 1.5 volts. A car battery has 12 or 24 volts.

The electrical power supplied in some countries, such as the United States and France, is about 115 volts. In the United Kingdom, the voltage is twice this, at 220 to 240 volts. Factories and industrial sites are supplied with much higher voltages, from 440 to more than 1,000.

Some of the highest voltages are found in the electricity supply cables that run underground or along pylons. These might be 30,000 volts, 110,000 volts or more.

The amount of electricity

The units called amps or ampères measure the amount of electricity flowing past a certain point within a certain time, usually one second. Amps are named after French scientist André-Marie Ampère (1775–1836). Just as the more water that passes through the pipe, the faster the bath or other container fills up, similarly, the more amps that pass through a wire, the greater the amount of electricity available to carry out work.

The power of electricity

Electricity's pushing force, in volts, and current, in amps, affect how much passes through a device or machine. This is known as the power of electricity—the amount of its energy made or used in a certain time. Power is measured in watts, named after Scottish engineer James Watt (1736–1819). A small electrical device such as a personal music player has just a few watts. A typical light bulb has about 60 or 100 watts. An electric heater might be rated at 1,000 watts, which is also called 1 kilowatt.

Center of power
Control rooms like this, in a big power plant, measure huge amounts of electricity, such as megawatts (millions of watts).

Flow and No-Flow

Electricity does not flow through air. At least, not usually. If it has a huge pushing force, in volts, it may be able to leap through air to a nearby object as a spark or discharge, such as lightning. Usually we make electricity flow where we want it to, by using an electrical conductor—a substance that carries current easily. In general, metals are good conductors. This is because their atoms have electrons that can easily move to other atoms, compared to those in nonmetal substances.

Electrical conductors

One of the best conductors is the metal silver. However, silver is too valuable to use in ordinary electrical wires and cables. The wires and cables used in our homes and in most other places are made from copper, another good conductor. But copper is too heavy to use in the thick wires and cables that are strung between pylons to carry electricity long distances across the country. These are generally made of the lightweight metal aluminum. The aluminum is usually mixed with other metals to form an alloy that carries electricity better than pure aluminum but is stronger and still lightweight. We will look at many other metallic alloys designed as conductors for special purposes, using rare metals such as niobium.

Some substances change the way they carry electricity, from fairly well to hardly at all, depending on conditions. These conditions include temperature, pressure, and the brightness of light. Such substances include silicon and germanium. They are known as semiconductors. As you will learn later, they are important in the electronics industry for making microchips.

Is water a conductor?

Pure water is a poor conductor of electricity. In daily life, though, water is rarely pure. Even tap water usually contains tiny amounts of dissolved substances such as salts and minerals. And even in tiny amounts, these substances make water a good conductor. This is why it is very dangerous to handle electrical equipment or to touch switches, plugs, and other electrical devices with wet hands or even in damp conditions. The water on the skin helps to conduct electricity into the body—which could be fatal.

Electrical insulators

Air is an insulator—it does not carry electric current well. Many other common substances are insulators, including glass, wood, paper and cardboard, pottery, natural fibers like cotton and wool, and most types of plastic. A typical electric wire has an inner core of copper or a similar metal as the conductor, and an outer covering of plastic as the insulator, to prevent the electricity from leaking away. Similarly, electrical machines and gadgets are usually contained in a casing made from an insulator, so we cannot receive a dangerous shock from the electrical parts inside.

Circuits

Electricity does not usually flow from its source, such as a battery or power plant, unless it has somewhere to go and come back again. This pathway for electricity is called a circuit. In a flashlight, the circuit runs from the battery, along a conductor, such as a metal wire or strip, to the bulb. Then it travels back to the battery again along another conductor. However, if the electricity flowed along this circuit all the time, the battery would soon use up all of its electrical energy and become discharged, or dead. So a special device is put into the circuit to create a break, or gap, in it. This stops the flow of electricity when the flashlight does not need to be lit. This simple device is called a switch. A diagram of a switch is shown on the next page.

Stopping and Resisting

Flowing electricity moves through a circuit only when it has an unbroken pathway through conductors, from its source and back again. When you plug an electrical device into a wall socket, you complete a very long circuit—from the power plant or the local electricity supply, all the way to your device, and back again.

Switch and resist
In this simple circuit, a switch turns the flow of electricity on or off. The variable resistor is adjusted to give less or more resistance. This makes the bulb glow brighter or dimmer.

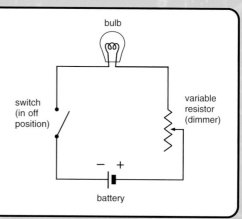

bulb

switch
(in off
position)

variable
resistor
(dimmer)

− +

battery

Switches

If this circuit is broken, by making a gap in it, the electricity stops flowing. This is the job of a switch. When the switch is on, it completes the continuous path for the electric current. Switching it off creates a break, usually in the form of an air gap between two ends, or contacts, of the conductors inside the switch. Air is a good insulator, and electricity cannot flow across it, so the current around the whole circuit stops.

Less flow

Conductors allow electricity to flow easily, while insulators do not. But there are different degrees of letting electricity flow. The opposition to its flow is called electrical resistance. It is measured in units called ohms, named after German scientist Georg Ohm (1789–1854). He showed that even a pure copper or silver wire was not a perfect conductor, while even a lump of wood did not have total resistance. The wire put up a slight resistance to the flow of current, while the wood had a huge resistance.

More experiments showed that longer wires have more resistance than shorter ones, and thicker wires have less resistance than thinner ones.

Fixed resistors

Devices called resistors are specially made to have an exact resistance, measured in ohms. They are usually shaped like small capsules or short rods, with colored bands. The colors show the resistance according to an international code. Resistors are part of most electrical circuits. They are used in gadgets ranging from personal music players to huge stadium sound systems. They adjust the amount of electricity for different components in the circuit, so they all work properly together.

Variable resistors

Electrical engineers today still use the basic rules figured out by Ohm and other pioneers of electricity. One common example occurs when we turn up the radio, television, or stereo, or when we change the lights with a dimmer switch. These devices use variable resistors, called rheostats. In a dimmer switch, the more the knob is turned up, the less the resistance in the switch. This means that more electricity can flow through, so the light shines more brightly. Volume controls work in the same way. As the controls are turned up, the resistance decreases, so more electricity can flow to the speaker for a louder sound.

Laws of electricity

One of the basic rules of electricity is Ohm's law. This simple formula links the resistance of a conductor in ohms, to the strength, or potential difference, of the electricity in volts, and the current, or amount of electricity, in amps. It says that the current passing through the conductor equals the voltage divided by the resistance:

$$I \text{ (current)} = \frac{V \text{ (voltage)}}{R \text{ (resistance)}}$$

Electrical engineers and circuit designers use Ohm's law and similar formulas all the time, to make sure all the wires, switches, and other components in a circuit are suitable. Otherwise they might overheat or burst into flames.

Circuits Galore

Only a few electrical devices have a simple circuit with only one pathway for electricity to flow. A flashlight is one example. From the electricity source (the battery) current flows to the switch, then to the bulb, and then back to the battery. Most circuits are far more complicated, with hundreds of components, or parts, and connections. But there are only two basic ways to join components together. These are called series and parallel circuits.

Series circuits

In a series circuit, all the components are joined one after the other, in a line around the circuit. There is just one route for the current to follow. The total resistance is figured out by adding up the resistances of all the various components. The strength, or voltage, of the electricity source, such as a battery, must then be enough to overcome this total resistance and push electricity all around the circuit. If one of the components fails, this makes a gap in the circuit. No electricity flows, and so all the components stop working.

Let there be light!
One panel controls the lighting at this sports stadium. The rows of lights connected into a parallel circuit all get brighter or dimmer together. Others, such as spotlights, each have their own individual circuits.

Parallel circuits

In a parallel circuit, the components are joined side by side, or in parallel to each other. It is like driving a car around a city. There are various routes to follow, and if one is blocked, this does not affect the others. Electricity tends to find the easiest route, with the least resistance. The total resistance is calculated by taking only a fraction of the resistance of each component. So it is much less than the same components connected in series. If one of the components fails, electricity can still flow through the others, along their own wires, and so they keep working.

Sources of electricity such as batteries can be connected in series or parallel. In a typical flashlight, two 1.5-volt batteries are linked in series. The total voltage they produce is 3 volts. The bulb of the flashlight must be suited to this voltage. If the batteries were connected in parallel, side by side, the total voltage they produce would be 1.5 volts. But they would be able to supply twice as much current, in amps, as the same batteries linked in series. What is gained in amps is lost in volts.

One for all, all for one

If a string of decorative lights is connected in series and one of the bulbs fails, all the bulbs go out. If the lights are connected in parallel and one of the bulbs fails, the other bulbs still glow. However in a parallel circuit, the total current flowing around the circuit stays the same. So each remaining bulb has to take an extra share of the current that would have flowed through the broken bulb. This means the remaining bulbs glow slightly brighter and get slightly hotter, making them more likely to fail. This is why, when one or two bulbs break and are not replaced, the rest may soon follow.

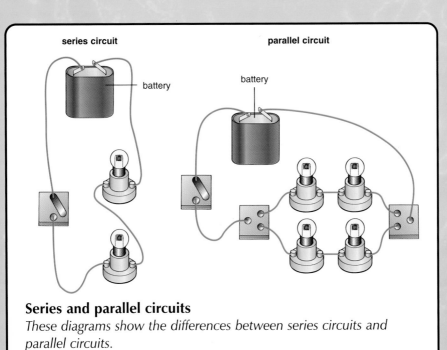

series circuit
parallel circuit
battery
battery

Series and parallel circuits
These diagrams show the differences between series circuits and parallel circuits.

Making Electricity the Chemical Way

There is a common electrical source that you can hold safely in your hand—the battery. A more accurate term for a battery is electrical cell. A battery is really several electrical cells joined together, but the term is now also used for single cells. A battery makes electrical energy from the energy contained in the chemical substances inside it.

Batteries for jobs

There are many sizes and shapes of cells and batteries. They use many different chemicals. Each type is designed to produce a certain strength, or voltage, of electricity, in a particular quantity, or current, for a certain length of time. Common voltages for batteries used in small devices are 1.5, 3, 6, and 9 volts. Car batteries have 12 or 24 volts. Low-voltage batteries can be connected in series so that their voltages add up. All cells and batteries have one feature in common: they make DC, or direct current. A very different kind of electricity supply is AC, or alternating current (see page 34).

Popular and portable

Early electrical cells and batteries were big, heavy, easily broken, and dangerous. They were filled with harmful chemicals such as strong acids. In the 1860s French engineer and chemist Georges Leclanché (1839–1882) devised a safer battery that could be carried more easily. His battery was a jar containing ammonium chloride solution and two electrodes. One electrode was a zinc rod. The other was a carbon rod inside a container of carbon and manganese dioxide powders. Leclanché's 1.5-volt cell was gradually improved into the standard dry cell or flashlight battery we use today.

Battery basics

A basic cell or battery has four main parts: a positive electrode, a negative electrode, an electrolyte (the substance between the electrodes) and a container, or casing. The electrodes are usually metals, such as copper and zinc, or substances with some metallike features, such as carbon. Often one electrode also forms the casing of the whole battery, while the other is a rod or strip. The electrolyte is between the two electrodes. It is often an acid, alkaline, or salt chemical. The electrolyte may be in liquid form, making it a wet cell or battery, or a gel, paste, or powder, making it a dry battery.

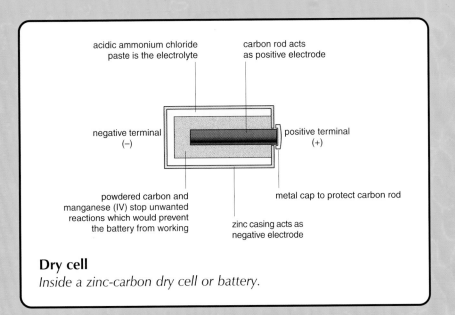

acidic ammonium chloride paste is the electrolyte

carbon rod acts as positive electrode

negative terminal (−)

positive terminal (+)

powdered carbon and manganese (IV) stop unwanted reactions which would prevent the battery from working

metal cap to protect carbon rod

zinc casing acts as negative electrode

Dry cell
Inside a zinc-carbon dry cell or battery.

Chemistry to electricity

When the battery is connected into a circuit, chemical reactions occur between the electrodes and the electrolyte. Electrons flow away from the electrode and around the circuit, to the positive electrode. This movement of electrons is the flow of electric current. As a cell or battery makes electricity in this way, it gradually uses up its chemicals and becomes weaker and finally dead. One way around this is to make the battery rechargeable (see next page). Another way is to use a fuel cell, which works similarly to a battery but continues making electricity, while also making hardly any pollution.

Hydrogen taxi
Fuel cells are devices similar to batteries that make electricity from a simple fuel such as water or the very light gas hydrogen. This experimental hydrogen fuel cell powers an electric taxi.

Storing Electricity

The fuel tank in a car is an energy supply, in chemical form, ready to be burned in the engine. A battery is a similar device. It is a supply of electrical energy ready to be used. When a car's tank runs low, it can be filled up with more fuel. So can a battery—but only if it is rechargeable. A primary battery or cell is not rechargeable. When it has used up its chemical energy, it is useless. A secondary battery or cell is rechargeable. Electrical energy is put in from another source, usually the main power supply. The energy makes the chemical reactions that originally produced the electricity work in the opposite direction. So the electrolyte and electrodes return to their original condition, ready to make electricity again.

Hybrids

A variation on the normal car or truck design is the hybrid vehicle. It differs from the usual design because the wheels are driven by electric motors. The batteries for these motors can be connected to the main electrical supply for recharging. But on a long trip, or when the main power supply is not available, a small gas or similar engine is used to turn a generator and supply electricity to recharge the batteries.

Big rechargeables

The main type of large rechargeable battery is called the lead-acid accumulator. This is the type of battery used in cars and trucks. The lead-acid accumulator has alternate plates of lead and lead oxide in a bath of sulfuric acid. The number of plates, or cells, determines the voltage produced—usually 6, 12, or 24 volts.

Lead is a very dense metal, and the whole battery is very heavy. However, it is one of the most reliable and long-lasting. It can supply a huge amount of electric current for a short time. This is needed in a car or truck to power the electric starter motor. The starter motor has to be powerful enough to get the whole engine turning for a short time before the engine can begin to work using its own fuel. Once the engine is running, it spins a generator attached to it that continually recharges the battery.

Small rechargeables

One of the main kinds of small rechargeable batteries is the nicad (short for nickel-cadmium). This battery usually has a nickel-plated steel canister as the negative electrode and a nickel-plated steel top cap for the positive electrode. An electrolyte paste on a spiral roll is between them. Nicads are useful in small electrical devices, such as laptop computers, personal music players, cell phones, handheld video games, toys, and small tools. The electricity to recharge them usually comes from a wall socket.

Muscle power

Some types of radios, flashlights, and other electrical devices run on a combination of mechanical and electrical technology. The mechanical part is clockwork. A long strip of metal formed into a spiral spring is wound up tight by a handle. As it unwinds slowly and steadily, it spins a small but powerful generator. This powers a recharger for the batteries. These wind-up devices can work for an hour or more on one minute of human muscle power.

Wind-up sound
Turning the handle charges the battery in this radio-flashlight.

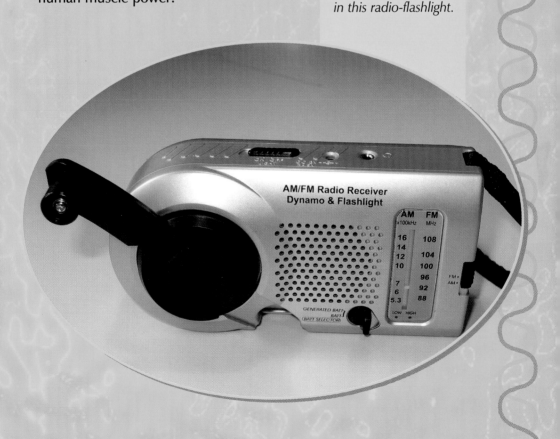

AM/FM Radio Receiver
Dynamo & Flashlight

AM	FM
x100kHz	MHz
16	108
14	
12	104
10	100
	96
7	92
6	
5.3	88

FM •
AM •

GENERATED BATT.
BATT.
(BATT SELECTOR)

LOW HIGH

Electric = Magnetic

Wherever there is electricity, there is also magnetism. They are two parts of the same type of energy or force, electromagnetism. This is one of the universe's most basic forces. These forces hold together, push apart, or move everything—from the tiny particles that make up atoms to whole stars and galaxies. For hundreds of years, electricity and magnetism were believed to be the same. The attraction to an object with electrostatic charge was thought to be no different from the attraction of a magnet to an object containing the metal iron.

One of the first people to look into how electricity and magnetism are related was Dutch scientist Hans Christian Oersted (1777–1851). He held a magnetic compass with its needle pointing toward the north near a wire carrying an electric current. The electric current caused the compass needle to point away from north. From his observation came huge advances in the science of electricity, including the invention of many of the machines and gadgets we use every day.

Electricity to magnetism

As an electric current flows through a wire or other conductor, it makes a magnetic force around the wire. This is called the electromagnetic effect. In most electrical wiring and cables, it is fairly weak. But winding the wire into a coil makes the magnetism stronger. Putting a rod of iron in the center of the coil makes the magnetism even stronger. This device is called an electromagnet. It has the features of an ordinary magnet, such as attracting objects containing iron. But the magnetism can be turned on and off by switching the electric current on and off.

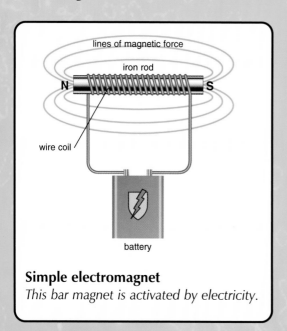

lines of magnetic force

iron rod

N   S

wire coil

battery

Simple electromagnet
This bar magnet is activated by electricity.

Magnetism to electricity

Just as electricity exists along with magnetism, the reverse is also true. Moving a magnet near a wire or similar conductor makes an electric current flow in the conductor. This is known as electromagnetic induction. However, the current flows only while the magnetism is moving relative to the wire, or while the magnetic field is changing or varying in strength. As soon as the magnetic field stops varying in strength, or stops moving in relation to the wire, the electric current stops flowing. Electromagnetic induction is used in many machines and devices in today's world, including generators, electric motors, and electric guitars. The guitar pickup has a strong bar magnet with a wire coil wound around it. The metal guitar string is close by. When the string is plucked and vibrates in the magnetic field, this alters its strength, which induces a tiny electric current in the wire coil. The current travels along the guitar lead to the amplifier and loudspeakers.

Current music
The electric guitar's barlike pickups under the strings work using electromagnetic induction.

How traffic lights work

How do traffic lights sometimes seem to know when to change as vehicles approach? Buried in the road are wires that carry a small electric current. The current creates a weak magnetic field above the road. As a car passes over, its metal parts disturb the magnetic field and change the current flowing through the wire. The change is picked up by the roadside equipment and used to control the lights.

Generating Electricity

A battery or electrical cell makes electricity from the energy contained in chemicals. A generator makes electricity from the energy of motion, called kinetic energy. Generators have many different designs and names, such as dynamos and alternators. But they all work in the same basic way. A magnet is near a coil of wire. A moving force turns one way or the other, and an electric current is created in the wire by electromagnetic induction.

Dynamos

In a simple dynamo-type generator, the coil of wire, called an armature, is on a shaft. It can spin around between the ends of a permanent magnet, where the magnetic field is strongest. The faster the coil turns, the more electricity is generated.

Dynamos like this are used on bicycles. The coil is turned by the cycle's rotating wheel, either by the tire at its rim or by the axle in its hub. The electricity generated is used to power the cycle's lights. One drawback is that when the cycle stops and the dynamo no longer turns, the electricity stops too and the lights go out. This can be overcome by using the dynamo to recharge a small battery that keeps the lights glowing even when the bicycle stops.

Wind to electricity
Almost any form of movement can generate electricity. In a wind turbine, moving air spins the large rotors (blades). These are linked to the generator at the top of the support tower. The energy created by the wind is harnessed to operate these generators.

Power plants

The generators in power plants are huge machines, sometimes as big as a row of houses. Most types use two sets of coils or windings, rather than one set, and a permanent magnet. One of the sets of windings is shaped into a huge ring and stays still. This is called the stator. The other set, the rotor, is mounted on a central shaft and turns around within the ring-shaped stator. Electricity is fed into one of the winding sets, usually the rotor. This turns the rotor into a powerful electromagnet. As its magnetic field spins, electricity flows through the windings of the stator by electromagnetic induction. The amount of electricity generated in the stator is far more than the amount fed into the rotor.

Sources of energy

The energy to spin a generator and make electricity comes from various sources. In some power plants, the source is a fuel such as gas, oil, or coal. It is burned to boil water into high-pressure steam. The steam blows past the angled blades of a huge turbine, like a circular fan. This makes the blades spin on their shaft, which is connected to the generator. In a nuclear power plant, heat from radioactive fuel boils the water. In a hydroelectric power plant, water from a river or behind a dam flows past the turbine blades to make them turn. In a wind turbine, or aerogenerator, the turbine is spun by wind blowing past its blades, like a windmill's sails.

Electricity in large amounts

The biggest power plants produce electricity in units of millions of watts, called megawatts, or MW. About 100 MW can power 50,000 homes.

Type of power project	Electricity produced
Large hydroelectric power project with many dams and turbines	over 12,000 MW
Large power plant fueled by coal, oil, gas, or nuclear energy	over 5,000 MW
Big solar power plant, making electricity directly from sunlight	over 100 MW
Big single wind turbine, or aerogenerator	3 MW

Using Electricity: Alternating

A battery produces a steady flow of electricity in one direction. This is called direct current (DC). The main supply of electricity to homes and other buildings is not DC. It is alternating current (AC). In an AC electricity supply, the current flows first in one direction, and then in the opposite direction. The flow alternates many times each second. The number of alternations in one second is called the AC frequency. It is measured in units called hertz (Hz), named after German scientist Heinrich Hertz. Most countries have an AC supply of 50 or 60 Hz, which means the electricity flow changes direction twice (one way, then the other) 50 or 60 times each second.

Radio pioneer

German scientist Heinrich Hertz (1857–1894) was the first person to show that radio waves existed, as predicted by Scottish scientist James Clerk Maxwell. Hertz made his first radio waves in 1888 using electrical sparks and built a detector that received them from 66 feet (20 m). He called them electric waves. Sadly, Hertz died of blood poisoning at the age of 36, just as Italian inventor Guglielmo Marconi was building improved radio equipment, to make radio a new form of instant long-distance communication.

AC vs. DC

Why is the electric power supply AC instead of DC? There are several reasons. One is that as electricity passes through a wire, it makes the wire warmer. This warmth is electrical energy lost as heat. The loss is greater with DC than with AC. In the same way that water flowing along a river rubs against the banks and wears them away, DC electricity "rubs" along its wire and heats the wire. AC moves back and forth in short bursts, so the rubbing effect is less. For this reason, using AC to send electricity long distances around a country in the electricity supply system is more efficient than using DC. Also the efficient and reliable types of electric motors used in many household appliances work only using AC, as you will learn later.

Around and around to up and down

Another reason why AC is used for electric power is the way generators work. The windings of the rotor produce a magnetic field that turns steadily within the windings of the stator. As the winding turns toward a magnetic pole, and then past it and away, the current changes direction. So as the magnetic field spins around and around, the induced electricity builds up to flow one way, then decreases and builds up to flow the other way, and so on. In other words, the electricity generated is AC. This type of generator is sometimes called an alternator.

Global electricity

The world's electric power is generated from these sources:

Coal	39%
Hydroelectricity	19%
Nuclear	16%
Gas	15%
Oil	10%
Other (wind, etc.)	1%

Upping the voltage

Another way of cutting energy losses when electricity is transported long distances is to make its voltage very high. This is known as high-tension electricity. Typical generators in power plants make electricity at around 20,000 to 25,000 volts. This is too low for long-distance travel, so the voltage is increased using a device called a transformer, as described on the next page. Transformers do not work with DC, which is another reason why the electric power supply is AC.

Electricity in transit
Long lines of pylons carry electricity across most modern countries. Some of these high-voltage power lines carry electricity at more than 500,000 volts.

Transforming Electricity

A transformer is a device that changes the voltage of electricity as well as its current, or amount of flow. In a power plant, a typical transformer design has two coils of wire wrapped around the same metal core. The core may be shaped like a bar, ring, horseshoe, or square. The two coils are not joined electrically. One, the primary coil, receives AC from the generator. As the current builds up and then fades, then does the same in the opposite direction, the coil works as an electromagnet to make a magnetic field in the core. The varying strength of the magnetism in turn produces a similar varying electric current in the secondary coil by electromagnetic induction. The secondary coil is connected into a different electric circuit. (Transformers cannot work with DC because it flows steadily and so would not produce the changing magnetic field needed to produce the current in the secondary coil.)

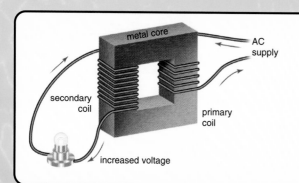

Transformer revealed
This diagram shows the primary and secondary coils that are the necessary part of an electrical step-up transformer.

Step-up

The strength of the induced electricity in the secondary coil depends on the number of turns in the two coils. If the secondary coil has five times more turns than the primary, the voltage in it will be about five times the voltage in the primary coil. So 20,000 volts from the generator will be stepped up to 100,000 volts. (It will actually be slightly less, because of energy lost in the transformer as heat and in other ways.) There is no overall gain of electrical energy, however. The voltage is increased five times, but the current is reduced by five times.

Step-down

Transformers come in many sizes and shapes, but they all work in the same way. Some increase, or step up, the voltage, mainly at power plants and electricity stations. Others decrease the voltage so that it can be used in homes, stores, and so on. These step-down transformers have fewer windings on the secondary coil than on the primary.

Everyday uses

More step-down or voltage-reduction transformers are familiar in daily use, as the rechargers for gadgets such as cell phones. These transformers plug into the main electric supply, 110 or 220 volts, and reduce it to 6 or 9 volts, or even less, for rechargeable batteries. Similar transformers are built into televisions and many other electronic devices. They supply the low voltages needed for the delicate electronic parts. They also convert the electricity from AC to DC by cutting off the current whenever it flows in one direction and smoothing it out when it flows in the other direction to fill the gap. Most delicate electrical circuits are designed to work using a steady supply of low-voltage direct current.

High-voltage sparks

Some of the highest voltages in everyday life are in our gas-engined vehicles. Spark plugs light the fuel inside the engine. To make the spark, a short burst of electricity is produced with an ignition coil, a device like a transformer, with thousands more windings on the secondary than the primary coil. It increases the car battery voltage, usually 12 volts, to an amazing sudden pulse of 20,000 volts or more to send to the spark plug.

Transformers
The step-up transformers at a power plant look like large ribbed metal boxes (shown here in the lower background).

Electricity to People

Electricity reaches our homes through a complicated maze of power lines, cables, transformers, and other devices. This is the electricity grid, or supply network. It links together many power plants so that they can share the job of supplying homes and buildings across a region, country, or whole continent. This allows a power plant to be off line and not generate when it needs servicing.

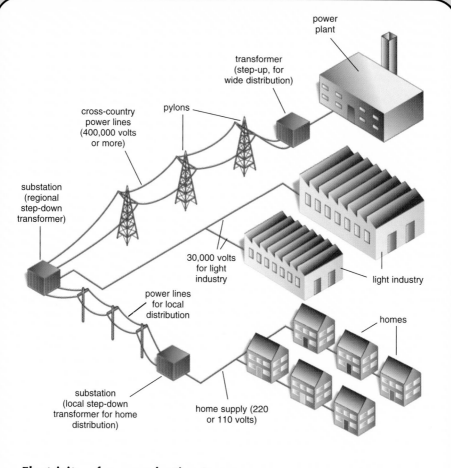

power plant

transformer (step-up, for wide distribution)

pylons

cross-country power lines (400,000 volts or more)

substation (regional step-down transformer)

30,000 volts for light industry

light industry

power lines for local distribution

homes

substation (local step-down transformer for home distribution)

home supply (220 or 110 volts)

Electricity—from production to users
This diagram shows how electrical power is distributed through a series of stations and substations, to light industry and to our homes. The whole system is monitored to warn controllers of any problems that may arise.

When the power goes off

A sudden increase in demand or a breakdown at a big generating station can overload the system and threaten a major power outage. Electricity engineers can increase the use of top-up generators. These are usually driven by gas turbine engines and can be running in a few minutes, delivering 100 MW or more each. Another option is brown-outs, in which the main voltage is reduced. Some electrical devices may not work, but the lights still do, although they may be dimmed.

Changing demand

Electricity demand rises in the morning as we get up, and again in the evening as we return home. And demand increases in cold weather as heating systems are switched on. Some heaters are powered by electricity alone. Others use oil or gas as fuel but still have electrical parts such as motor-driven pumps. Power plant generators cannot be switched on and off like light bulbs. They are huge, complex machines—the rotor at the heart of a generator weighs as much as a jumbo jet and spins 50 or 60 times every second. A big generator may take a day or more to warm up to full working condition. So at times of low demand, generators may still run, but their electricity goes unused.

Ups and downs

In a typical supply network, power plants generate electricity at about 22,000 volts AC. This is stepped up by huge transformers at the power plant to 400,000 volts or more, for long-distance transmission. Electricity travels along power lines strung between pylons, under the ground, or even under the sea. The electricity is carried to a major substation, where step-down transformers reduce its voltage to 275,000 or lower, to send it out to several destinations along thinner power lines.

Reaching the users

The next stage is the area electricity substation, where the voltage is reduced again, perhaps to 33,000 volts. Some of this supply is sent directly along power lines to big users such as factories and electric railways. The rest is sent to neighborhood transformer substations. Here the power can be reduced to 660 or 440 volts or thereabouts, for smaller factories and farms, and to 110 volts (in the United States and Europe) or 220 volts (in the United Kingdom), for homes.

Electric Motors

One of the most widespread uses of electricity is to drive electric motors. A motor does the opposite of what a generator does—it changes electrical energy into motion, or kinetic energy. Motors run all kinds of household tools and appliances, and the motion they usually produce is turning or spinning. In some we can see the spinning, as in a washing machine. In others, such as the water pump in a central heating system, the movement is less obvious. There are two basic types of electric motors. One works using DC, the other using AC.

DC motor

When electricity flows through a wire coil, it makes the coil into an electromagnet. If there is another magnetic field nearby, the electromagnet's field may interfere with it and produce attraction and repulsion forces. In a typical DC motor, the wire coil is on a shaft and spins within the field of a permanent magnet around it. As the motor starts, electricity flows through the coil, turning it into a magnet. The magnetic north pole of the coil's field is nearest the north pole of the permanent magnet. The two repel, making the coil turn, because its north pole is attracted to the south pole of the permanent magnet.

Reversed flow

As the coil turns on its shaft and its north pole comes close to the south pole of the permanent magnet, the electricity flowing through the coil is reversed. This is done by a commutator, a spinning switch made of two half-rings on the shaft. The commutator touches pads or brushes that bring the DC to the coil. The commutator is positioned on the shaft so that it switches the direction of current at precisely the correct moment. The coil's reversed electricity makes its north and south poles reverse, while the permanent magnet's poles stay the same. The coil's north pole becomes a south pole, and is repelled by the south pole of the permanent magnet. The coil is made to spin another half turn. The commutator then reverses the electric current again, and the cycle continues.

Many coils

The account above describes a simple electric motor, with one coil and a commutator made of two half-rings. Most electric motors have a series of coils mounted around the shaft, and a commutator with many parts.

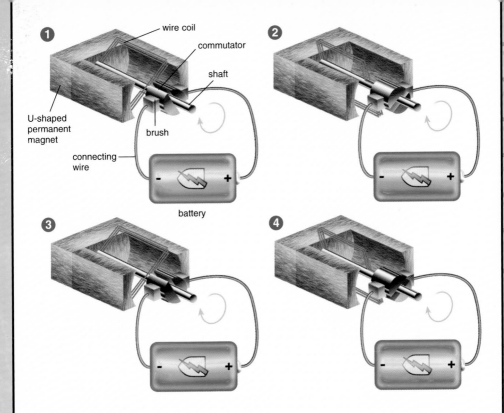

Simple DC motor

The rotating switch, called the commutator, changes the direction of current twice during each turn. This is explained in more detail on these pages.

The electricity to the coils is switched one way and then the other several times with each rotation. This makes the turning motion much smoother.

DC motors are used in battery-powered devices such as hand-held cooling fans, portable CD players, and toy cars and trains. They are also used in devices such as computers that are powered by AC from the main supply, but that contain transformers and other equipment to produce low-voltage DC for their electronic circuits.

Efficient energy change

Electric motors are, in general, a very good way of producing motion from another energy source. Most are able to change over 70 percent of the electrical energy put into them into the energy of motion. Some types are over 90 percent efficient. This is far better than a gas-powered car, in which only 30 to 40 percent of the energy put into it as fuel is turned into the energy of motion to make the car move.

More on Motors

Switch on a common household appliance, such as a vacuum-cleaner or washing machine, and you may set off the type of AC motor called an induction motor. It has no commutator or brushes to wear out, and looks like a miniature version of a power plant generator. The first AC motors were designed in the 1880s by Croatian-born American scientist Nikola Tesla. Along with other advantages of AC, as previously explained, they were a major reason why the main electricity supply is AC rather than DC.

Spinning magnetism

The AC induction motor has a series of windings, forming a ring-shaped stator. The stator surrounds the windings of a rotor on a shaft. Alternating current is fed into the stator windings and produces a magnetic field that rotates from one set of windings to the next, around and around the stator. The stator's moving magnetic field makes electricity flow in the coils of the rotor by electromagnetic induction. This induced electricity turns the rotor into an electromagnet too. As the magnetic field of the stator rotates, it drags the magnetic field of the rotor with it, making the rotor spin.

Motors galore

The typical AC induction motor runs at a constant speed, according to the current's frequency or speed of change. By supplying a DC motor with a higher or lower voltage of electricity, it is easy to make it turn faster or more slowly. The turning speed of some AC motors can also

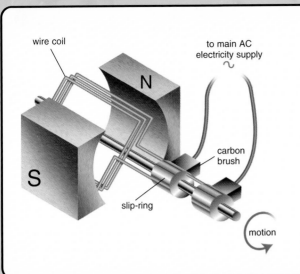

wire coil

to main AC electricity supply

N

S

carbon brush

slip-ring

motion

be altered using electronic circuits. There are also electric motors smaller than pin heads, for miniature electrical equipment, while the motors that drive electric trains are as big as family cars. Some motors are designed to rotate at incredible speeds, thousands of times every second. The motor of a computer's hard disc spins it 100 times per second or more.

The electric car

Electric motors are usually quiet and efficient at turning electrical energy into movement. They also do not produce air pollution. In these features they differ greatly from gas and diesel engines. So why are there so few electric engines? A major problem is the limited distance they can travel using the energy in their batteries. Recharging takes several hours—much longer than filling a tank with gasoline or diesel fuel.

Ready to stop
Electric cars tend to accelerate less rapidly and cruise more slowly than gas-powered cars.

All-Electric Lifestyle

A typical home has over 100 electrically powered devices, machines, and appliances, from simple light bulbs to complex computers. Some use tiny amounts of electricity, while others consume hundreds of times more.

Electricity around the house

The electricity supply to a house usually arrives along a thick cable, the main, to a box called a consumer unit. This has meters to measure the amounts of electricity used. Each electrical device does not have its own wires connecting it to the consumer unit. Instead, about six to ten separate circuits run from the consumer unit around the building, and the devices connect into them. Lights do not use much electricity, so lighting circuits are designed for low currents such as 15 or 20 amps. The circuits for the sockets in the walls can carry more current, 30 amps or greater.

Cook electric

A kitchen has many electrical appliances, from the oven and refrigerator to battery-operated salt- and pepper-mills.

Ring circuits

These lighting and wall-socket circuits are usually called ring mains. A cable runs from the consumer unit to each light or socket in turn, and then back to the consumer unit, forming a ring. This means electricity can flow to a light or socket both ways around the ring, which cuts the current carried by the cables in half and stops them from overloading. Big electricity users such as electric stoves or water-heaters have their own circuits.

Saving electricity

Making electricity uses up valuable resources and causes huge amounts of pollution. Saving it helps to reduce these problems and saves money, too. Be aware of wasted electricity around the home. Turn off lights in unused rooms. Turn TVs and stereos off if you are not watching or listening. Do not stand in front of the open refrigerator while you decide what kind of snack you want. If you have electric heat turn down the temperature a few degrees and wear a sweater.

Safety

There are several safety features built into a house's electricity system. One is the grounding connection. If the wires inside an electrical appliance came loose, they might touch the metal casing of the appliance. Then if a person touched this casing, she or he would receive a very dangerous electric shock, which could kill. So the casing is connected to a wire called the ground. If a fault does occur, this wire carries the electricity away harmlessly into the ground. At the same time a safety device called a circuit breaker detects any leak of electricity along the ground wire. The circuit breaker is usually in the consumer unit, and it breaks the circuit or trips—cuts off the electricity supply. In older consumer unit designs, a fuse did a similar job. The fuse contains a very thin piece of wire to carry the current. If too much electricity tries to flow along it because of a fault, the fuse heats up, the wire melts, and the circuit is broken.

Electrical usage

One kilowatt (1 kW) of electricity would power these devices for the following average lengths of time:

Electric twin oven: 20–30 minutes
Microwave oven: 30–60 minutes
Vacuum cleaner: 45–90 minutes
Hair dryer: 30–50 minutes
Standard electric heater: 1 hour
Big-screen television: 3–5 hours
Standard light bulb: 10 hours
Small television: 10 hours
Low-energy light bulb: 30–50 hours

Electronics

The difference between electric and electronic is partly one of scale. Electric involves the flow of electrons in large quantities, usually millions and billions at a time. Electrical devices are often partly mechanical, too, with moving parts, and some use other types of energy as well, such as heat. Electronic devices, such as microchips, use much smaller amounts of electricity with fewer electrons. They also rarely have mechanical moving parts. They are sometimes described as solid-state. This means that all their operations happen within a solid object, with no mechanical moving parts.

Semiconductors

Most electronic devices are based on semiconductors. Semiconductors used for electronic circuits are normally made of silicon, germanium, or cadmium sulfide. However, the name *semiconductor* is slightly misleading. A semiconductor may allow electrons to flow very easily, like a conductor, or it may resist their flow, like an insulator, depending on the conditions. One important condition is temperature. A semiconductor acts as an insulator until its temperature rises to a certain point. Then with a further rise in temperature of just a tiny fraction of a degree, it changes or, flips, and carries electrons well, becoming a reasonable conductor. This feature is used in electronic or digital thermometers to measure temperature very accurately.

Transistors

One of the most useful electronic devices is the transistor. The transistor was invented in the 1940s by a team including William Shockley (see box). It can do several jobs. For instance, it can work as a switch or make an electric current oscillate or alternate—flow first one way, then the other. A transistor can also amplify an electric current, or make it stronger. How does it do this? The transistor uses the up-and-down variations in a tiny electrical current to control a much larger current and make it vary up and down in the same way. This is how the tiny electrical signals from a microphone or electric guitar are made powerful enough to feed into loudspeakers to produce sounds.

Integrated circuits

Many electrical parts, reduced to a microscopic scale, can be put on a thin wafer, or chip, of semiconductor. These parts include the equivalent of wires, switches, resistors, capacitors, transistors, and many other larger parts. They are all integrated—that is, produced already connected together in position, rather than being built up piece by piece, like an ordinary electrical circuit. These integrated circuits, or ICs, also called microchips, are the basis of many modern electronic machines. A microprocessor is a chip that contains all the parts needed to carry out, or process, a complete task or computation, such as adding numbers.

Smaller and smaller

William Shockley (1910–1989), along with John Bardeen and Walter Brattain, developed the transistor in the late 1940s. It was far smaller and lighter, less fragile, and used less electricity than a similar device invented in the 1900s, the thermionic valve. Radios, televisions, and similar devices quickly became much smaller and more reliable. Shockley worked with small crystals of germanium and silicon. The three scientists received a Nobel Prize for their achievements in 1956.

How small can they be made?

Every year, electronics engineers figure out new ways to squeeze more, smaller components and devices onto a microchip. The first home-computer microprocessor, introduced in 1974, had the equivalent of 8,000 transistors on one chip. The latest microprocessors pack in more than 40 million transistors, and they work a thousand times faster, too.

Deep inside a chip
Magnified many thousands of times, a tiny section of a microchip reveals the hundreds of transistors and other components on its surface.

Electronic Machines

Two of the most familiar electronic machines are the television and the computer. Both rely on moving and manipulating electrons to show words and pictures on their screens. In a standard screen (not flat-screen type), there is a large pear-shaped container called the tube, usually made of glass. The flattened wide end forms the screen. At the thinner end are devices called electron guns. Electron guns are charged with such high voltages of electricity that electrons leap, or fire, from them. The electrons are not fired into air, because there is none inside the tube. All the air has been removed to form a vacuum.

Electron guns and beams

The electrons are fired rapidly, like machine-gun bullets, along the tube to hit the inside of the screen at the other end. Billions of electrons are fired every second. Each burst of electron fire is called an electron beam. They hit the inside of the screen, which is coated with special chemicals called phosphors. When electrons strike the phosphors, they glow with light. We see the light from the other side of the transparent screen as the glow of the image.

Dotty screen
This close-up of TV screen pixels shows how the image is made up of many tiny dots of three main colors.

48

Flat-screen technology

Newer plasma screens are shaped not like tubes, but like flat boxes that can be hung on the wall. The screen is made up of thousands of tiny boxlike cells, arranged in a grid system like windows in a skyscraper. Each cell contains a gas and an electrode. When the electrode is given an electric charge, this makes the gas burn for a split second, changing it into a form called plasma. The plasma gives out energy as ultraviolet light (see next page), which hits a patch of phosphor in the cell and makes it glow in the same way as happens in an ordinary TV screen. This happens in thousands of cells many times each second, building up the image over the whole screen.

Glowing spots
A plasma screen, like this one, has thousands of tiny boxes in which gas glows for a split second to make a spot of light.

Deflecting the beam

The direction of the electron beam is controlled by electromagnets, or electrically-charged plates, around the middle of the tube. The beam itself is made up of electrons, so it has a negative charge. As it passes an electrically charged plate that is positive, it is attracted to the plate. So it bends toward it slightly before heading on to the screen. A negative charge deflects, or pushes away, the beam.

Scanning

The plates make the beam deflect sideways, to spray electrons in a line across the top of the screen. The beam then makes another line just below this one, and so on, line by line down the screen. This is called scanning. It happens so fast, usually covering the screen in less than one twentieth of a second, that we do not notice the image building up. As soon as it is complete, the scanning starts again to form a new image. The many separate images per second merge to give the impression of constant movement.

Digital Electricity

Digital technology is everywhere—in computers, CDs, DVDs, digital audio tape (DAT), and digital television and radio. Older technology, called analog, deals with electricity that varies constantly, up and down, like the peaks and troughs of waves. Digital equipment does not use up and down, but on and off.

A very short pulse of electricity stands for the digit (number) 1, while the lack of a pulse stands for 0. The number system that uses only these two digits, 1 and 0, is called binary. It is the basis of computer technology. Binary digits, known as bits, can be combined in longer sequences of 4, 8, 16, and so on, known as bytes. This allows information to be carried in coded form, by on-off pulses of electricity. The pulses happen very fast, millions per second, and they can be sent along wires and through microchips to stand for letters, words, colors, sounds—anything.

Computer innards
A weak X ray scanning beam, as used at baggage security checks, shows circuits and components inside a laptop computer. X rays are a type of electromagnetic wave.

Digital TV and radio

Digital technology is replacing analog, especially for television and radio broadcasting. The on-off pulses of electricity happen so fast, they can carry far more information than the up-and-down waves of analog systems. The same radio waves that carry one television channel in the analog format can carry between five and ten channels in the digital format. Some telephone systems have become completely digital, while others still have analog technology.

Computers

Nearly all computers use digital technology. The letters of words, the numbers of math, the shapes and colors of an image, the loudness and pitch of a sound, and any other forms of data or information are all turned into the 1s and 0s of binary code. Inside the computer, binary code is in the form of tiny electrical pulses and no-pulses. The brain of the computer is the central processing unit, or CPU. In the CPU, the information is changed according to the computer's program.

Electrical waves

Electricity cannot pass through air, at least not in the form of an electric current. But the effects of combined electricity and magnetism can pass through air, in the form of the varying electrical and magnetic fields that make up electromagnetic waves. The air around us is full of these invisible waves. They include a whole range of waves with different wavelengths, from very long to very short. All these waves together are known as the electromagnetic spectrum. We know some parts of the electromagnetic spectrum by familiar names—radio waves, microwaves, light waves or rays, and X rays.

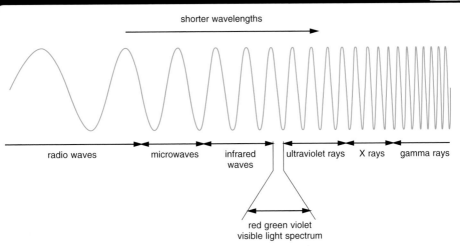

shorter wavelengths

radio waves | microwaves | infrared waves | ultraviolet rays | X rays | gamma rays

red green violet
visible light spectrum

Many waves
The whole spectrum of electromagnetic waves ranges from radio waves, where each wave can be hundreds of yards or meters long, to gamma rays, where billions of waves stretch less than 0.04 inch (1 mm). Variations in the height or length of the waves carry information in analog format. On-off pulses of the waves can carry information in digital format.

Summary: an Electrical World

The science of electricity can become very complex. It involves measurements such as volts, amps, watts, and ohms; many different substances that are insulators, semiconductors, or conductors; and an almost endless list of devices such as resistors, capacitors, rectifiers, and transistors, which are combined into a vast array of circuits and networks. There are various ways of transferring and transforming electricity, and of storing it and making it. Electrical machines fill factories and mass production lines. Many of them make more electrical machines—goods and appliances that work by electricity, from toasters to clothes dryers, digital cameras to home-entertainment centers.

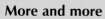

More and more
Millions of electrical devices, like these washing machines, are produced every day.

Supply and demand

Providing electricity for our homes, offices, schools, and factories is a huge business. There are meters to read, which keep track of how much electricity we use, and payments to make for its supply. Keeping people safe from electricity is also very important, since it can be deadly. Electrical experts constantly discuss and update rules and laws, for example about the designs of plugs and sockets, and new inventions, such as the latest cell phones.

Vital to modern life

Yet electricity is so simple and easy to use that we hardly ever stop to think about it. We flick on a light switch, turn on the television, listen to music, or tap away at a computer keyboard without a thought for the complicated electrical circuits and components being used. Only when we have no electricity, during a power outage or in a remote place with no supply, do we understand how important this form of energy is for our modern world and our daily lives.

Glossary

alternating current (AC) flow of electricity that changes direction, usually many times per second

alternator generator that makes alternating current (AC)

amp unit of the amount of electricity flowing

amplify make bigger, larger, greater, or more powerful

analog working by continuously changing or varying amounts (compare digital)

battery group of electrical cells joined together, making electricity from chemicals

capacitor device that stores electrical charge

cell single device for making electricity from chemicals (several joined together are a battery)

chip microchip, small slice of semiconductor carrying millions of microscopic electrical components

circuit route around which electricity flows

commutator a type of switch that turns around on an axle or shaft, to reverse the direction of the electric current in a motor

conduct carry electricity, heat, or sound

conductor substance through which electricity, heat, or sound can pass

digital working in small separate steps or stages (compare analog)

direct current (DC) flow of electricity in one direction only

discharge lose electrical charge (from an object or substance)

dry cell/battery electric cell or battery in which the chemicals are in the form of a paste or solid

dynamo generator that produces direct current (DC)

ECG electrocardiograph, device that shows the electrical signals in the heart

EEG electroencephalograph, device that shows the electrical signals in the brain

electrode contact or object through which electricity flows into or out of a conducting substance

electrolyte substance, usually a liquid or paste, through which electricity passes between electrodes

electromagnetic force combined electrical and magnetic energy

electromagnetic induction producing electricity using magnetism

electrons subatomic particles with a negative charge

farad measure of capacitance, or store of electrical charge

fuel cell device that produces electricity by oxidizing a fuel

generator device that changes motion energy to electricity

ground route for electricity to flow away safely, usually down into the ground

hertz unit of frequency, used, for example, in measuring the rate of change in direction in alternating current

ignite set fire to, light with a spark

induction motor motor that uses alternating current (AC) and the principal of electromagnetic induction

insulator material that reduces the flow of heat, sound, or electricity—a poor conductor

integrated circuit small electrical device with components produced already in position and connected together (also called microchip or chip)

ions atoms or similar particles with positive or negative charge

main electricity electricity from the wall sockets of a typical house, usually 110 or 220 volts

motor (electric motor) machine that turns electricity into the energy of motion

neutron subatomic particle with no charge found in the nucleus of an atom

ohm unit for measuring resistance of a substance to flow of electricity

parallel (of electrical components) connected side by side so electricity flows through both at the same time

potential difference difference in energy between two parts of an electric circuit

proton positively charged subatomic particle found in the nucleus of an atom

resistor device or substance that holds back the flow of, or resists, electricity in a precise way

rotor in a generator or electric motor, a coil of wire or group of coils that rotate

semiconductor device or substance that partly allows or partly resists the flow of electricity, depending on conditions

series (of electrical components) connected one after the other in a circuit

static electricity electrical charge that builds up on an object as electrons are either rubbed off or deposited onto it

stator in a generator or electric motor, a coil of wire, or group of coils, that stays still and does not rotate

temperature measure of how cold or hot something is

transformer device that changes the voltage in an electrical system

volt unit for measuring the strength or push of electricity (potential difference)

watt unit of power

Further Reading

Books

Baker, Wendy, Alexandra Parsons, and Andrew Haslam. *Make it Work! Science: Electricity*. Princeton, NJ: Two-Can Publishing, 2000.

Fullick, Ann. *Groundbreakers: Michael Faraday*. Chicago: Heinemann Library, 2000.

Hewitt, Sally, and Catherine Ward. *Fascinating Science Projects: Electricity and Magnetism*. New York: Franklin Watts, 2002.

Hunter, Rebecca. *Science, The Facts: Electricity*. New York: Franklin Watts, 2003.

Oxlade, Chris. *Science Topics: Electricity and Magnetism*. Chicago: Heinemann Library, 1999.

Parker, Steve. *Eyewitness: Electricity*. New York: DK Publishing, 2000.

Index